EARTHQUAKES

SEYMOUR SIMON

MORROW JUNIOR BOOKS
New York

ILLUSTRATION CREDITS

Photo Researchers, Inc., © Richard Nairin, p. 32; Terraphotographics/BPS,
© John K. Nakata, pp. 30-31; all other photographs courtesy of the
National Geophysical Data Center/NOAA. Drawings on page 8 by Ann Neumann;
maps on pages 11 and 12 by Arlene Goldberg.

The text type is 18 point Garamond Book.

1 2 3 4 5 6 7 8 9 10
Library of Congress Cataloging-in-Publication Data
Simon, Seymour.
Earthquakes / Seymour Simon.
p. cm.
Summary: Examines the phenomenon of earthquakes, describing how
and where they occur, how they can be predicted, and how much damage
they can inflict.
ISBN 0-688-09633-6.—ISBN 0-688-09634-4 (lib. bdg.)
1. Earthquakes—Juvenile literature. [1. Earthquakes.]
I. Title.
QE521.3.S54 1991
551.2'2—dc20
90-19328 CIP AC

To my grandnieces and grandnephews:

Bryan, Dena, Debbie, David, Alex, Michael, and Daniel

The earth beneath our feet usually feels solid and firm. Yet a million times each year—an average of once every thirty seconds—somewhere around the world the ground shakes and sways. We call this an earthquake.

Most earthquakes are too small to be noticed by people; only sensitive scientific instruments record their passage. But hundreds of quakes every year are strong enough to change the face of the land. A medium-sized earthquake near Seattle, Washington, bent these railroad tracks into twisted ribbons of steel. A larger earthquake can cause enormous destruction.

On the morning of September 19, 1985, a major earthquake struck Mexico City. It killed ten thousand people and injured another twenty thousand. Hundreds of buildings were destroyed, including homes and stores, hotels and hospitals, and schools and businesses. This multilevel parking garage (center left) collapsed like a house of cards, while some of the neighboring buildings suffered only slight damage.

BLOCKS AT REST   STRESS BUILDS UP ALONG THE FAULT   THE ENERGY IS RELEASED

Most earthquakes take place in the earth's crust, a five-to thirty-mile-deep layer of rocks that covers the earth. Cracks in the rocks, called faults, run through the crust. The rocks on one side of a fault push against the rocks on the other side, causing energy to build up. For years, friction will hold the rocks in place. But finally, like a stretched rubber band, the rocks suddenly snap past each other. The place where this happens is called the focus of an earthquake.

From the focus, the energy of the quake speeds outward through the surrounding rocks in all directions. The shocks may last for less than a second for a small quake to several minutes for a major one. Weaker shocks, called aftershocks, can follow a quake on and off for days or weeks.

Sections of the crust have slipped past each other along two fault lines and offset this ridge in Wyoming (left). This kind of sideways movement is called a strike-slip fault.

Sometimes one side of a fault will slip higher than the other. This is what happened along this highway in the Mojave Desert of California (right). This kind of up-and-down movement is called a dip-slip fault.

Four out of five of the world's earthquakes take place along the rim of the Pacific Ocean, a zone called the Pacific Ring of Fire. Alaska, California, Mexico, the west coasts of Central and South America, and the east coasts of China, Japan, and New Zealand are all located within the Pacific Ring of Fire. Another major earthquake zone stretches through Italy, Greece, and Turkey to the Middle East and into Asia.

In the United States, almost half of the quakes each year occur in southern California. In other sections of the United States, earthquakes are rare. About the only places that have never recorded an earthquake are the southern parts of Florida, Alabama, and Texas.

Earthquake Zones in the Continental United States

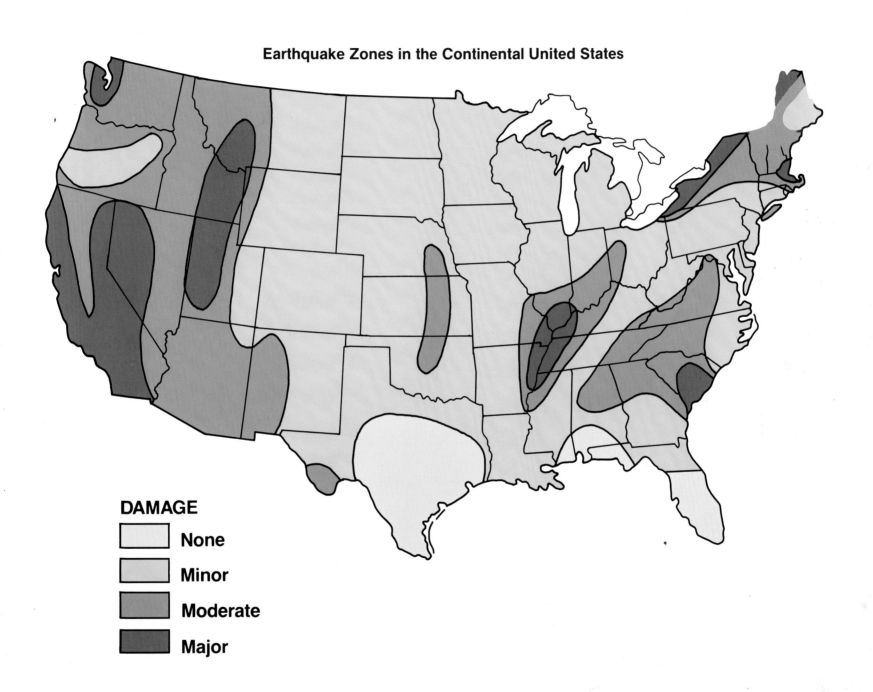

DAMAGE

	None
	Minor
	Moderate
	Major

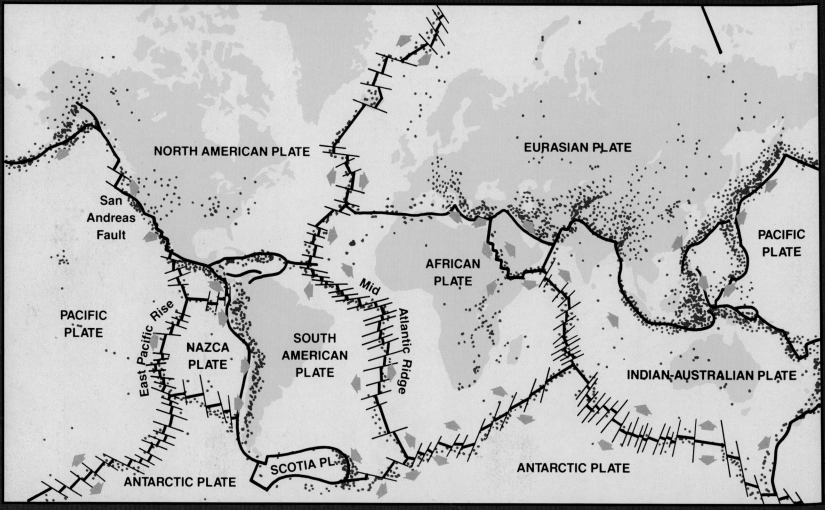

This map shows the plates in the earth's crust. The red dots indicate places where earthquakes have occurred.

Why do most earthquakes in the United States occur in California? The answer lies deep within the earth. The earth's solid rocky crust floats on the mantle, an 1,800-mile-thick layer of very heavy, melted rock that moves up and down and around. Over the years, these movements have cracked the crust like an eggshell into a number of huge pieces called plates.

The plates float slowly about on the mantle up to four inches a year. As the plates move, they run into or pull away from each other, producing enormous strains in the rocks along their edges. The United States and Canada are riding on the North American plate, which is slowly moving into the Pacific plate. The colliding plates are what causes most of the earthquakes along the West Coast. But earthquakes can occur anywhere there are stresses in underlying rocks.

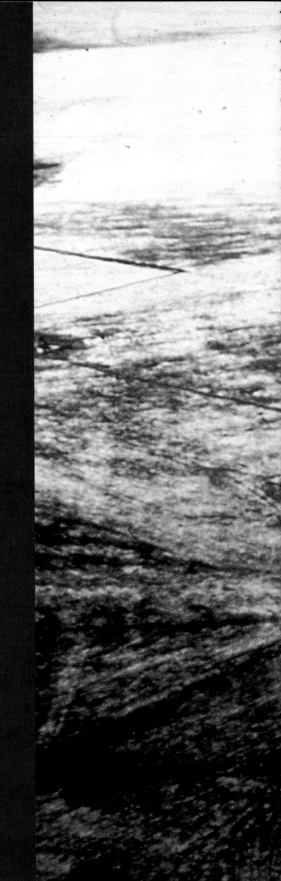

The San Andreas Fault is the boundary line between the North American and the Pacific plates. It winds seven hundred miles through southern California to just north of San Francisco, where it dives under the Pacific Ocean. Along the way, it slashes under houses and dams, across deserts and farms, and through towns and cities where more than 20 million people live. Dozens of small- to medium-sized quakes occur along this fault each year. Scientists think that a huge, deadly earthquake will strike along the San Andreas Fault by the end of this century.

The 1906 San Francisco earthquake was one of the most violent earthquakes ever recorded. The gigantic quake was felt over an area of 375,000 miles, more than twice the size of California. More than three thousand people lost their lives in the quake and the following fires. This view shows San Francisco in flames hours after the quake. The fires alone destroyed 28,000 buildings in the city.

This fence was broken and offset eight feet by the movement of the San Andreas Fault during the 1906 earthquake. Besides the widespread strike (side-to-side) slip along the fault, there was also a dip (up-and-down) slip of as much as three feet in some places.

How do you measure and compare the sizes of earthquakes? The size cannot be judged solely by the damage to buildings or the number of people killed. That's because a medium quake close to a large city will cause more destruction than will a larger quake in an unpopulated area.

Seismographs are the instruments that scientists use to measure earthquake shocks. A modern seismograph (right) can record a tiny earth tremor thousands of miles away. The tremor shows as a wiggly line traced on a turning drum. The bigger the quake, the larger the wiggle.

There are hundreds of seismograph stations all over the world that time the arrival of earthquake waves. Scientists use the measurements to find an earthquake's force, its focus underground, and its epicenter, the place on the ground just above the focus.

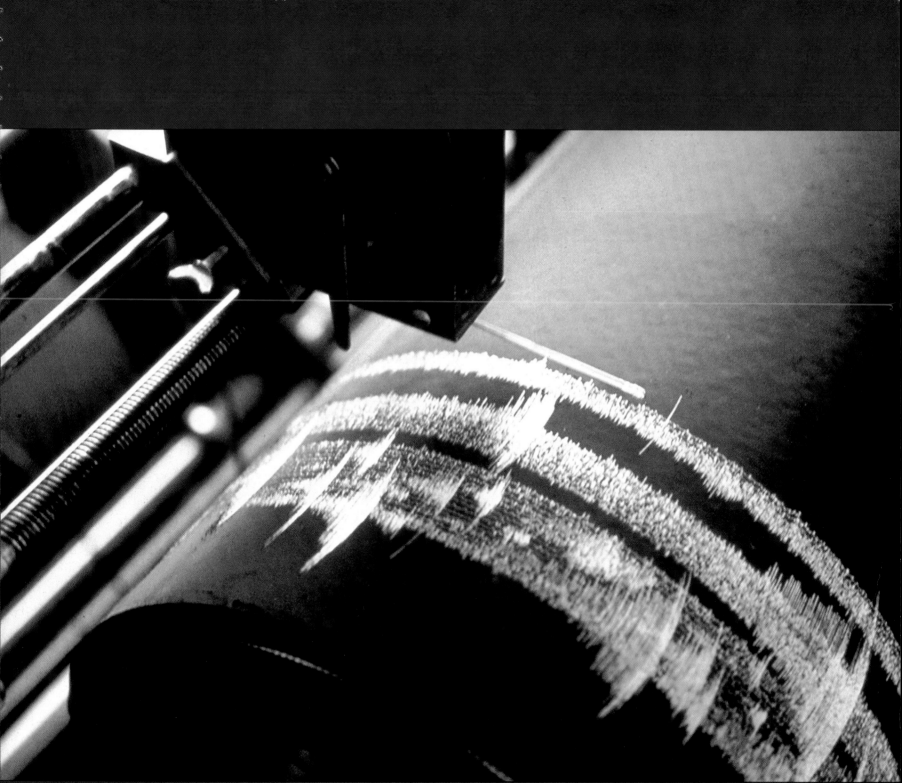

Scientists use the Richter Scale to measure an earthquake's magnitude, the amount of energy it releases. Each number on the Richter Scale stands for an earthquake that is ten times more powerful than the number below it. You would hardly notice a magnitude-2 quake, but a magnitude-3 quake is ten times greater and easily felt by everyone. The scale has no upper end, but any quake that registers 6 or more is considered a major quake.

The Armenian earthquake of December 7, 1988, measured 6.9 and was followed, four minutes later, by a 5.8 aftershock. Dozens of other quakes occurred in the area over the next months. The quake and aftershocks caused tens of thousands of deaths and injuries, terrible destruction, and made half a million people homeless.

Scientists use another scale to measure the effects of an earthquake. The Mercali Intensity Scale uses observations of the quake damage to rate it on a scale ranging from I, where the effects are scarcely noticeable, to XII, where damage is total and the ground heaves in waves. Usually, the intensity is greatest near the center of the quake and smaller the farther away from the center. But other factors, such as the soil in the area and the construction of the buildings, are also important.

For example, the earthquake that shook the San Francisco area in October 1989 (during the World Series) measured 7.1 on the Richter Scale. On the Mercali scale, it measured X to XI in the Marina district (shown here), where the houses are built on loose soil, but only VI or VII in other parts of the city, where the houses suffered much less damage.

Sand sometimes bubbles up during earthquakes, gushing water and soil like miniature mud volcanoes. These "sand boils" are particularly dangerous to buildings. In places where water is close to the surface, sandy layers turn into quicksand and structures crumble. During the 1989 San Francisco quake, sand boils erupted in basements, yards, and beneath houses all over the Marina district.

These apartment houses in Niigata, Japan, tumbled as a result of an earthquake in 1964. The leaning buildings were caused when the soil beneath the foundations turned to quicksand. About a third of the city sunk by as much as six feet when the soil dropped away.

On the afternoon of Good Friday, March 27, 1964, Anchorage, Alaska, was shaken apart by the most violent earthquake ever recorded in the United States. It measured 8.4 on the Richter Scale. Government Hill Elementary School was split in two when the ground beneath it dropped. Houses began sliding apart, cracks in the pavement opened and closed like huge jaws, the ground rolled in huge waves. In the first three days after the quake, three hundred aftershocks shook the buildings that remained standing.

The Good Friday earthquake brought another type of destruction along the coastline. The focus of the quake was deep beneath the waters of Prince William Sound in the Gulf of Alaska. The quake acted like a giant paddle churning the waters.

Huge quake-formed sea waves, called tsunamis, battered the land for hours. An entire section of the waterfront at the port of Seward cracked off and slid into the ocean. Boats were overturned, buildings broke apart, and everything was left in a tangled mess.

The tsunamis moved across the Pacific at speeds of hundreds of miles an hour, reaching as far as Hawaii and even Japan, four thousand miles away.

Scientists have learned much about earthquakes and their effects. They can measure even the slightest movements along faults. But we need to know much more about earthquakes before we can predict weeks or even days in advance when a big one will hit. Until then, proper building design can help lessen their effects. We now know that houses in earthquake-prone areas should be built on solid rock and not on sand, for example. In California and Japan, new houses are designed to be earthquake-resistant.

It also helps to know what to do when an earthquake strikes. If you are indoors, get under a heavy table, desk, or bed. Stay away from windows, mirrors, or high cabinets. If you are in a high building, stay out of the elevators and stairways. If you are outdoors, move away from high buildings, walls, power poles, or any other tall objects. If possible, move to an open area. Above all, remain calm and don't worry. The chances of your being hurt in a quake are very, very slight.